COLOR BY NUMBER - UNICORNS, MERMAIDS & CO.

A FUN COLORING BOOK FOR KIDS

FUNKEY BOOKS

You can find more of our books
on Amazon!

Simply search for "Funkey Books"
on www.amazon.com.

Hi there _____!

Awesome that our little book has found its way to you. This is going to be fun!

So let's get to some coloring!

Each picture in this book is divided into shapes and has a unique coloring key going along with it. The key is there to help you figure out which color each little field should have. If the color of pencil number 1 is "blue", for example, every shape with the number 1 on it can be colored in blue.

Little tip: Don't press your coloured pencil as hard for the lighter colors as you would for the darker ones to achieve different color effects.

And, of course, we don't want to limit your imagi-nation. So if you think that some elements would look nicer in a different color or if you don't have a specific color, don't worry: Just take another one and your picture will look just as beautiful!

Now bring each page to life with some color and - most importantly - enjoy! :-)

Let's go!

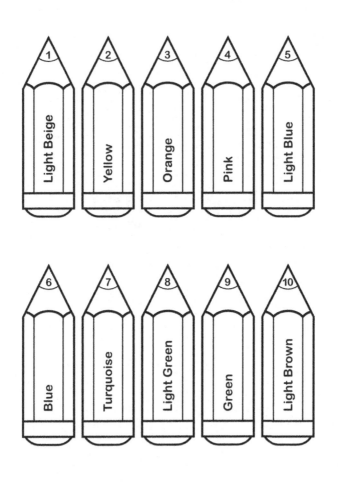

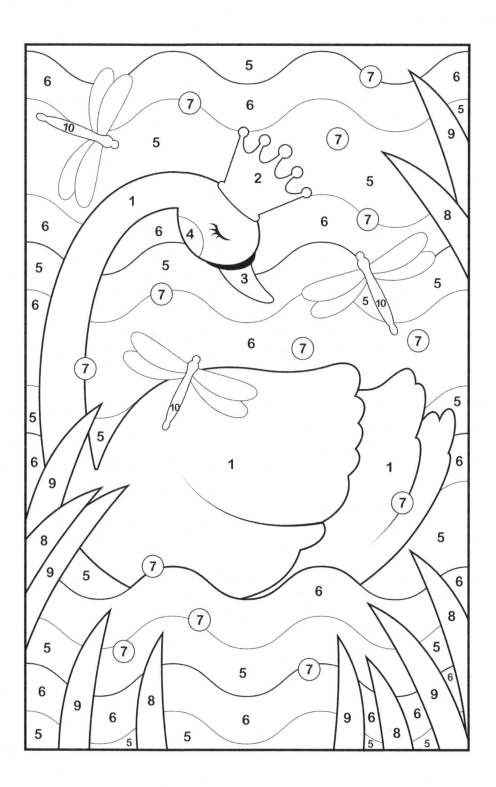

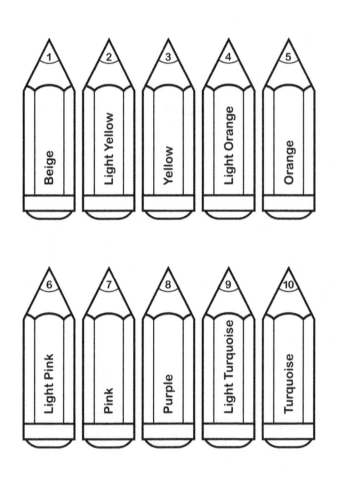

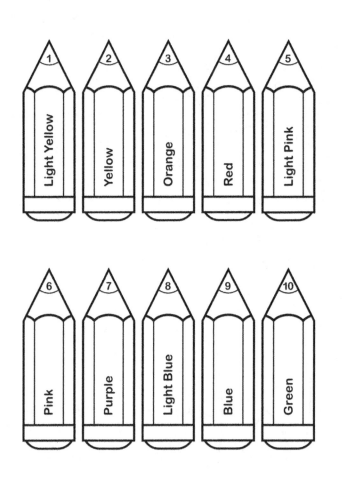

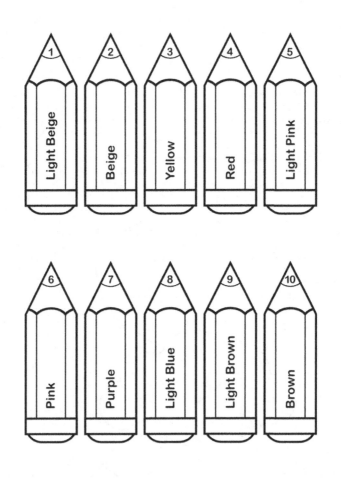

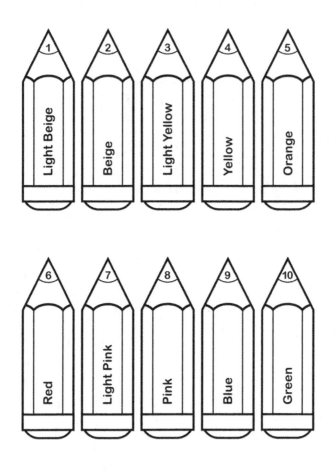

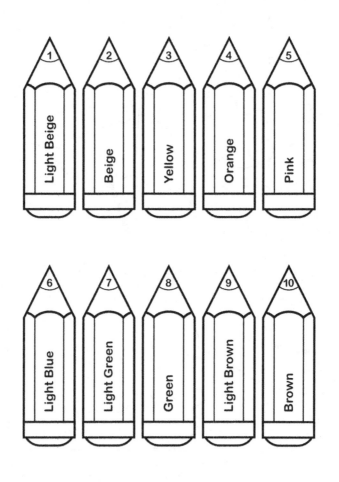

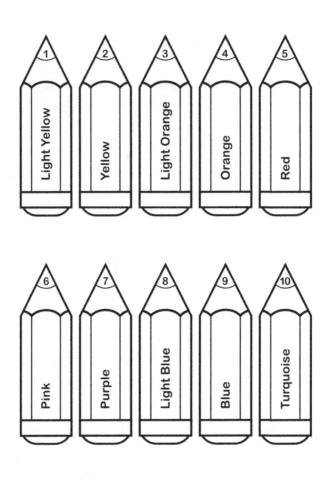

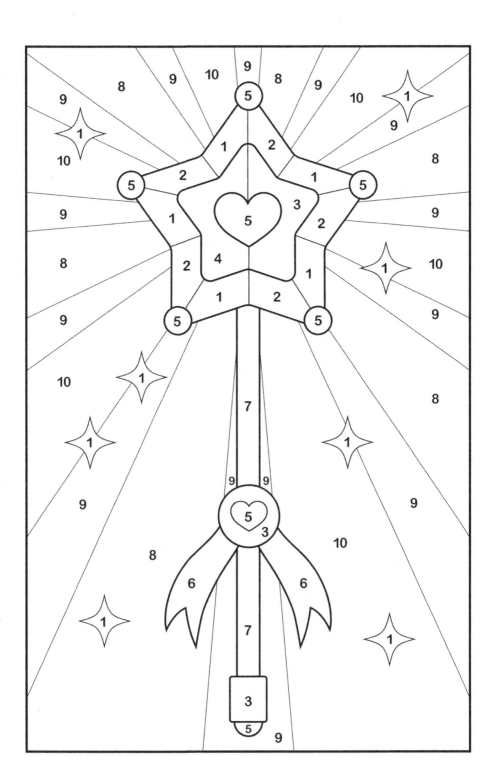

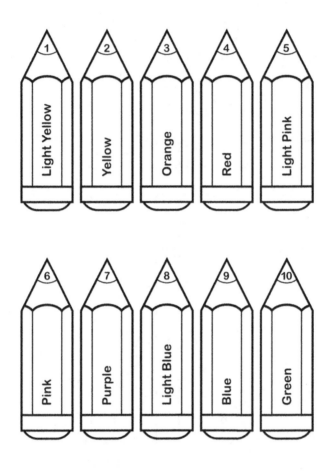

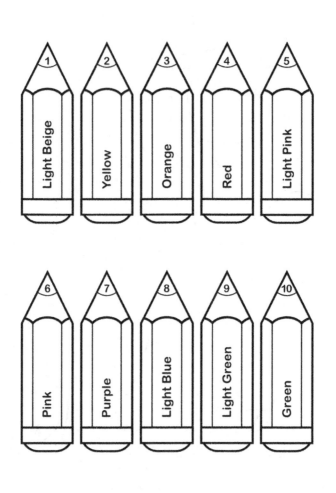

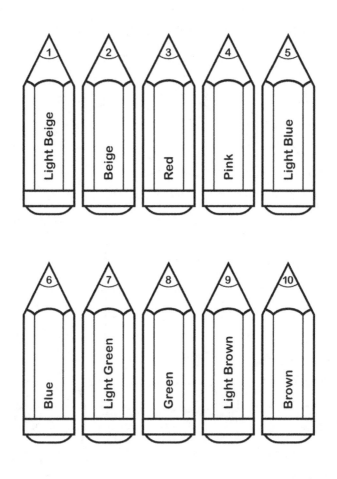

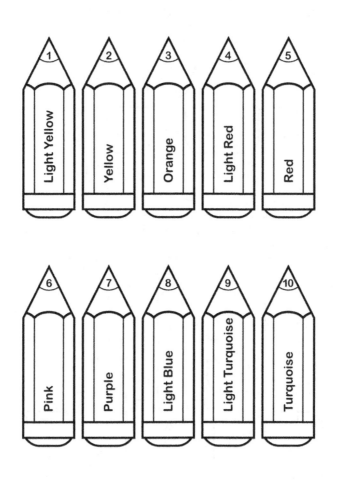

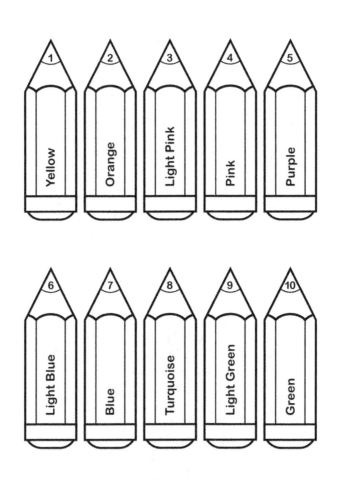

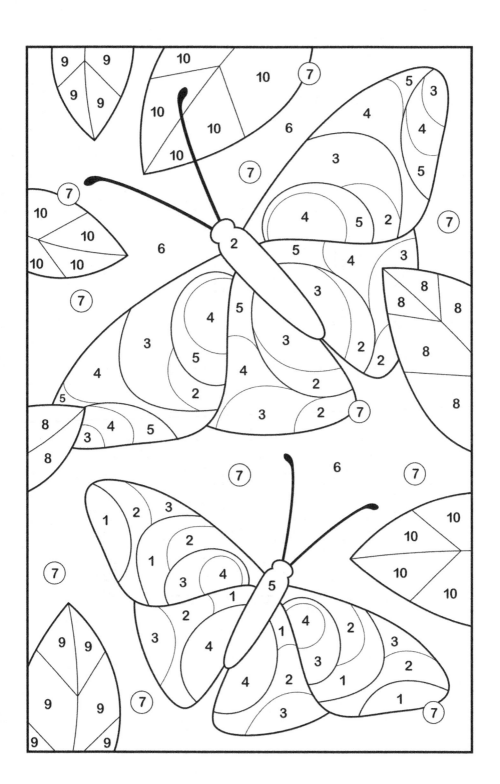

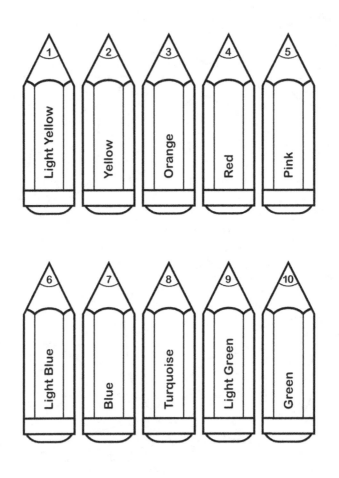

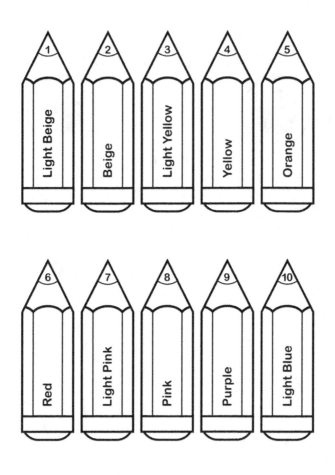

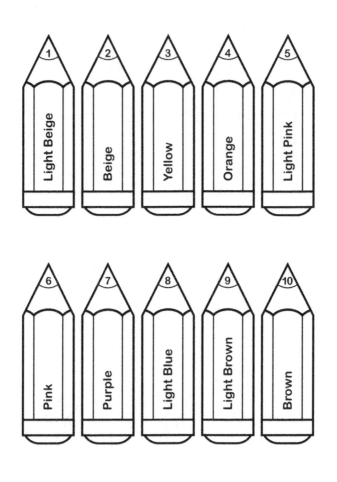

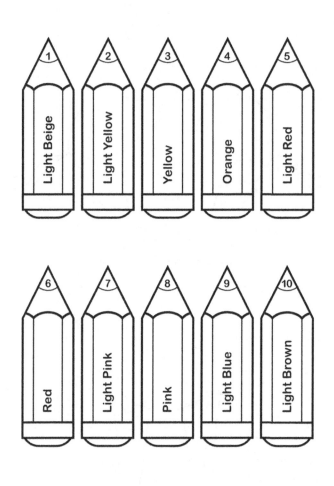

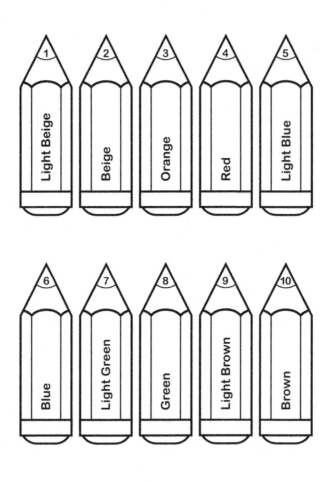

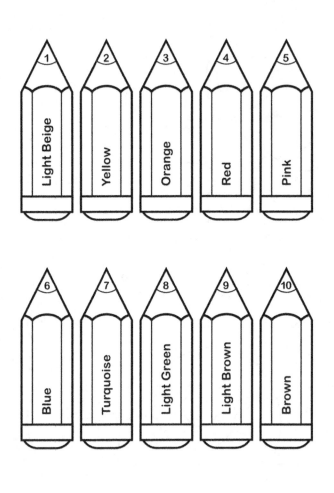

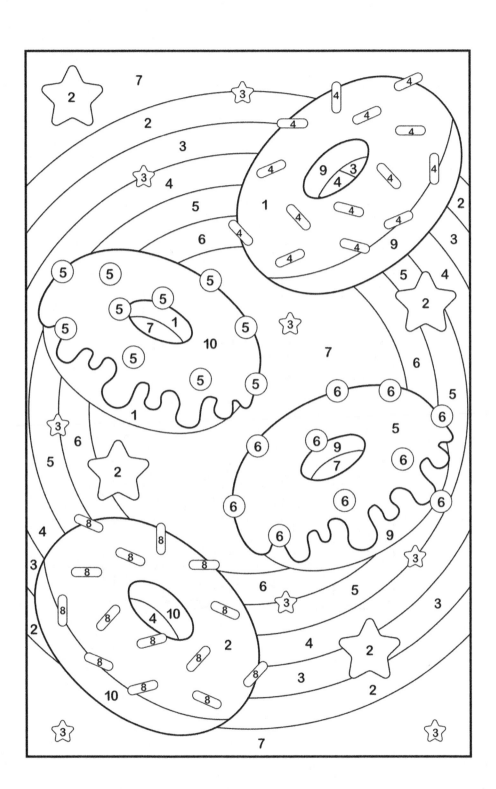

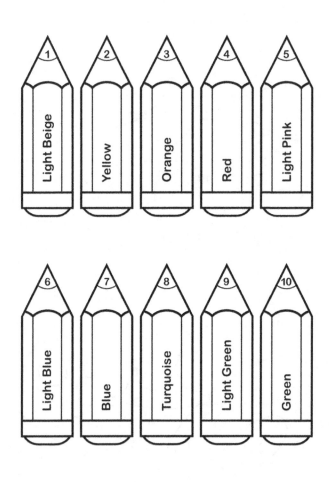

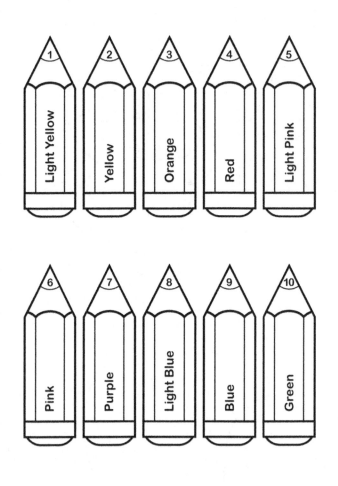

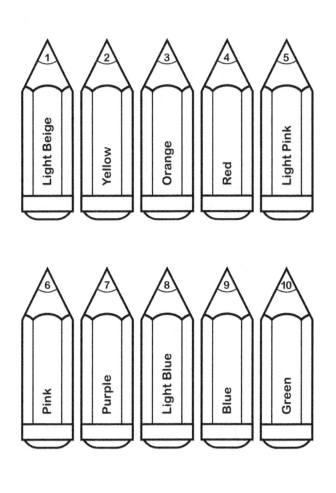

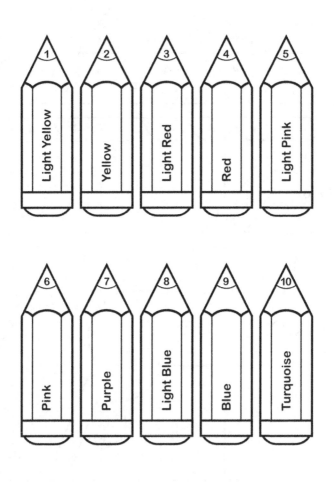

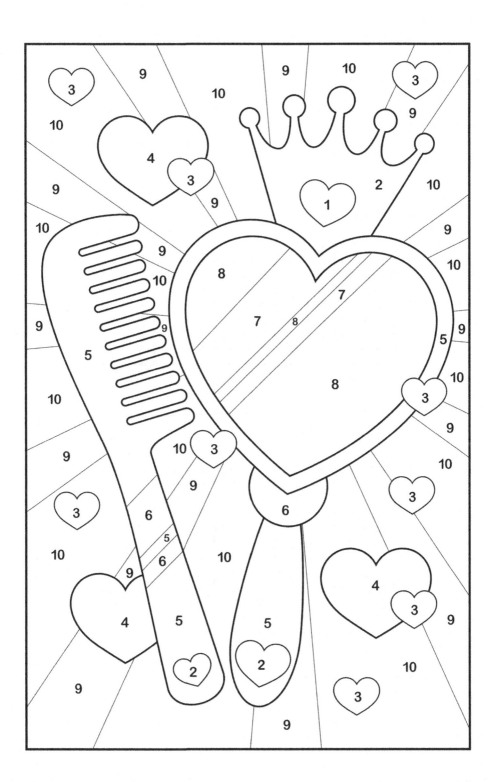

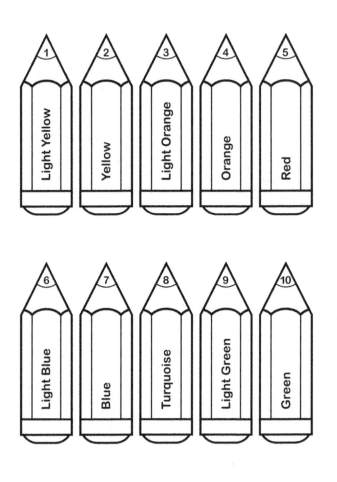

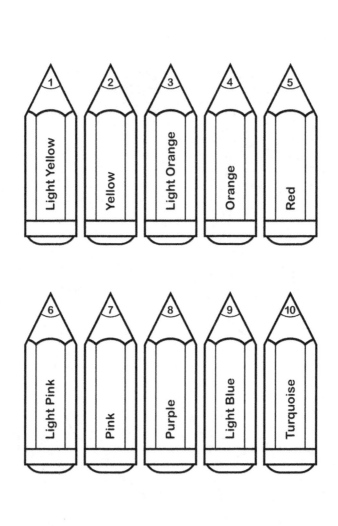

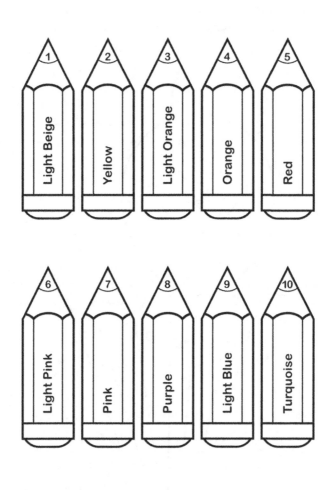

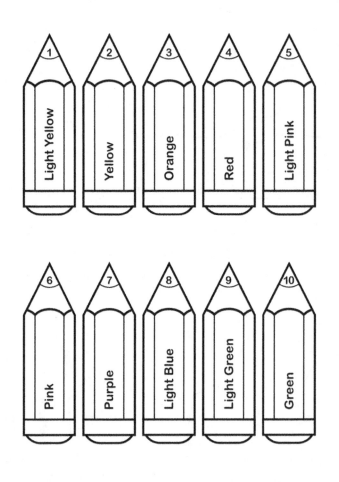

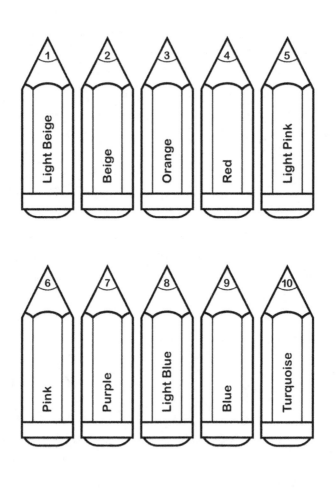

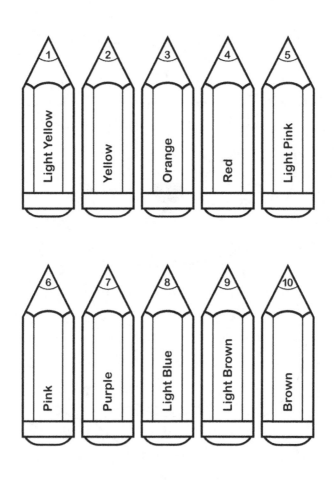

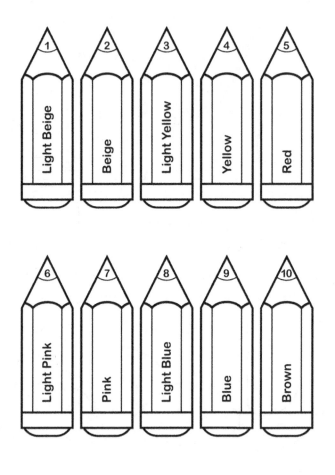

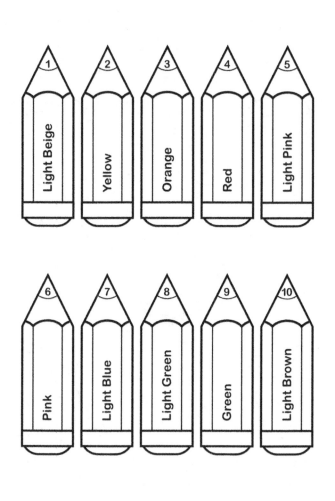

WOW! Great Work!

You colored in all of the pictures and brought
this little book to life.

Very impressive stuff!

If you enjoyed working through the pages,
we would love to hear about it.
You can do this by leaving a review wherever
you purchased this book. We really appreciate
getting feedback from our little colorers.

Thank you very much, and have
a fantastic day!

Made in United States
North Haven, CT
17 June 2023

37898644R00039